CHOOSING A GUEST

Also by Michael Schmidt

POETRY
Black Buildings   1969
Bedlam & the Oakwood   1970
Desert of the Lions   1972
It Was My Tree   1972
My Brother Gloucester   1976
A Change of Affairs   1978

TRANSLATION
Flower and Song (with Edward Kissam)   1977

FICTION
The Colonist   1980

ANTHOLOGIES
Ten English Poets   1976
Eleven British Poets   1980
Some Contemporary Poets   1983

CRITICISM
An Introduction to Fifty Modern British Poets   1979
An Introduction to Fifty British Poets: 1300-1900   1979

CRITICAL ANTHOLOGIES
British Poetry Since 1960 (with Grevel Lindop)   1972
British Poetry Since 1970 (with Peter Jones)   1980

Michael Schmidt

Choosing a Guest

NEW AND SELECTED POEMS

Anvil Press Poetry

Published in 1983
by Anvil Press Poetry Ltd
69 King George Street London SE10 8PX
ISBN 0 85646 105 9

This book is published
with financial assistance from
The Arts Council of Great Britain

*Printed in England at
The Arc & Throstle Press
Todmorden Lancs.*

ACKNOWLEDGEMENTS
Some of the 'New Poems' have previously appeared in *Critical
Quarterly, The London Review of Books, Poetry Durham* and
The Yale Review.

FOR CLAIRE

This selection of fifty-seven poems is drawn from four published collections and includes a section of recent work. New work has been put first, but thematically it grows out of the work at the end of the collection. This book does not represent 'all the work I wish to retain' from my earlier collections, but rather what I take to be the better poems and those which make thematic or formal connections.

Michael Schmidt
April 1983

CONTENTS

New Poems (1978-82)
'Under the great stone Churn . . .'   *11*
'The cattle's hill is tall . . .'   *12*
Faith   *13*
The Road   *14*
The Swallows   *16*
The Pond   *17*
A Phrase of Dryden's Virgil   *18*
In a Darkening Thicket   *19*
What He Saw   *20*
A Savage Dream   *21*
For My Father   *22*
The Ground   *23*
Adam   *24*
Ariel   *25*
Caliban   *25*
Habit   *26*
Elsewhere   *27*
Choosing a Guest   *28*
Jacob   *29*
Objections   *30*
Vigil   *31*
Recovery   *32*
The High Rooms   *33*

from *Bedlam & the Oakwood* (1970)
Inside the Mapmaker's Mind   *37*
Mr James   *38*
Convento del Carmen: Mummies   *39*
Carlotta at Borda   *40*
If a Frog Can Swallow its Eyes . . .   *41*

from *Desert of the Lions* (1972)
Underwater   *45*
Away   *47*
Scorpion   *48*
'Indian Pipes' Are Flowers   *50*
The Well at Balankanche   *52*

from *My Brother Gloucester* (1976)
The Judas Fish   *57*
Writing   *59*
Words   *60*
My Town   *62*
The Fool   *64*
The English Lesson   *66*
The Sleigh   *67*
Natalya's Dream   *70*
Wasps' Nest   *72*
The Shells   *73*
The Freeze   *75*

from *A Change of Affairs* (1978)
A Dream   *79*
The Brother   *81*
Absalom   *82*
A Carol   *83*
Sisera   *85*
Augustine   *86*
'Until I built the wall . . .'   *87*
Choice   *89*
A Change of Affairs   *90*
'I make no secret of it . . .'   *91*
Waking and Sleeping   *91*
Piano   *93*
Here and There   *94*
The Honeysuckle   *95*

New Poems
(1978-82)

Under the great stone Churn with its hoop of shale
That ticks all winter like a giant clock
And sends down sheets of rock a hundred feet
Into our unwalled orchards that stay sweet
With fallen fruit until spring sours them —
Under the Churn I grow up and then old
All in a year, and sit here on the soil
Wrapped like a caterpillar in my rugs
But am unchanged and do not hope to fly.
Only the eye scales the steep air, the ear
Calls down the lonely birds and focuses
In age and silence, in their solitude,
Whatever being has been scattered, multiplied,
And the dropped shale seems written with some news,
The language strange, implicit, that I read
But can translate not even into words.

Neighbouring is the walled yard of the church.
My trees overhang and are drawn down
By green-black ivy so they feed the dead
Red fruit and little leaves, a dust of blossom.
It will not be hard to climb the dry stone wall
And add a life to those four centuries:
My trees send their long heavy branches over
To feel a way for me, and so repay
My care, as they did my father's and his father's:
They are my hands and the dark ivy holds them.

The cattle's hill is tall and near the top
Ungrazeable, sunned granite starred with gorse,
But the herds ascend even the narrow ways,
Pause at the summit, noses to the ground.
Later and leaner they come down
To the deep grass, to the dark barn.

When I cannot believe,
The brown herds still move across green fields
Into the tufty hills, and I was born
Higher, where I could watch them as a bird might.
When even memory seems imagined, what
Can I bring to prayer? A pair of knees.
The great faith that built a stair to heaven
As now my memory tries to climb a hill,
Becomes an old stone building, a deaf priest
Whose hand is in the pockets of his parish,
Who longs to buy a bell he'll never hear.
The water in the font is cold, I trace
A circle on my brow and not a cross.

The road is long and flat.
Where does it intend?
To where the sky's blue lip
Seals with the darkening ground.

Here a milestone names
A town before nightfall.
And the name! The name of the town
Is like the name of a girl.

I fall in love with the name
And with the speck of a spire
That at each footfall grows
Out of the plain expanse.

It focuses the eye,
Makes vacancy a scene.
Before the roofs appear
I people the unknown streets —

There moves every desire
A lonely walker owns.
I mouth the name like a prayer.
Milestones answer for her.

Perspective is reduced
Until both earth and sky
Are lost in the approach.
I see the first pale lamps.

It is the name I love,
And seeds I plant in the name.
A spangled silhouette,
The first smells of the town.

Here is the outer gate,
A dog, a beggar, and small
The houses are, and the spire
Sounds one clanking bell.

Brisk with certainty,
I choose the principal street
Looking for the heart
And still obtuse with love.

And that was the town. Ahead
The road is long and flat
To where the sky's dark lip
Seals with the darkening ground.

The swallows circle, when will they come down?
I have prepared a place for them, and grain.
Sun has warmed the stones, the foliage sweats,
Casting exact shadows. It is noon.

Noon and then afternoon, the stretching light
Climbs through ivy, up the trellises
And gradually it leaves a pool of shadow
Where I stand looking up, and still the swallows

Circle. I have waited
Below, and in my hand
Have elevated seeds for them and stood
Still as a tree heavy with sweet fruit.

Now I resign, I am a man again.
I throw the grain onto the flags and breathe
Deeply as the darkness grows. And now
The swallows, one by one, descend.

There were no willows but there was a pond
Steep at the edges where I sat and stared
Past my reflection, deep into seeming light.

As I grew older, so the carp grew large,
Green among weed or gold, or turned
A silver belly up; in autumn brisk,

While in the summer they lay stunned, inert.
A child might drown in such a pond, I heard.
Watching there, for a time I was a child.

One summer it was hot for days and days.
Green skin spread on the water, water-weed
Broke through the surface, and at last the bed

Began to parch, what little damp remained
Was stagnant and then mud in which the fish
Pulsed gracelessly, snared like wingless birds.

No more reflections then: I walked among
The large fish that for years had drawn my eye
And saw them take the air to heart, and how

They urged their bodies under the wilted weeds
And died. Incurious birds
Dropped from the air among them, finding food.

Too late the rain came, and I saw my face
Again on water, rippled by a breeze
Or on calm days whole and staring deep

Where water-weed revived but wore a light
Now literal and creatureless.
In such a pond a child might drown.

All was the night's he wrote. All
Was the night's. I cannot add
A word. I go
Along a gravel path
Between shrubs sick with rose scent
And on the pool a shimmering bough of starlight
Marks the easy entrance to the dark.

My voice lost, the thicket growing dark,
Are they all gone? Only my lips say *Fetch me.*
Night settles, round and perfect as an egg.

If I wave a handkerchief it will be a shadow
Like a bat caught in a web, and there are not even stars
— The gesture of Icarus, his mess of feathers
White on the sea as the foamy cap of a wave.

How far they have moved off — I hear them laughing,
Breaking their ways through, home, in all directions.
No one says *Where is he? He is always slow,*
Or looks over a shoulder into the dark
Calling my name. They are all blind as I
But go together, talking, while I stand
Afraid not of danger or the place,
But my companions receding like a tide.

Brittle the wood when I move against the twigs,
Brittle the match I strike on my shoe
To see the darkness darker round the glow.
I cup the light in my hand against the breeze
And know that they will find me if I touch
This trembling stem and this with fire. How far is home?
Will I see the distant windows in the glare
And my companions wait at the open door?

The bullet struck him. He was standing by a tree.
Keep still, he told himself. He laid his hand
Upon the bark and rigid as the dead
He stood until the leaves fell, the snow fell.
Never felt pain. Never felt the wound
Which movement would acknowledge. He kept still
As the dead when it struck him and he saw
Behind closed eyes not what the dying see —
A life re-run before the darkness clouds —
But what would follow him: the leaves, the snow.

A SAVAGE DREAM

I had a savage dream of destinations:
A ten-foot fence, barbed, and on the wire
Bones and the rags of prisoners. I had
This dream, and woke in the cool English air.

FOR MY FATHER

I learn the dead wear shoes.
Their beards cast a last shadow.
Kissing your face,
I'm troubled by the roughness
As when you came to tuck me up,
Brushed my cheek with yours
And tip-toed out.

THE GROUND

Because I have no curtains in my room
And these country nights are dark as they are cold
Reflections frame me when the lights go on
— As a fish sees the pond surfaces
Repeat, reversed, the green
Familiar weed and sand made strange and clear
So that it rises to graze there
And chills its lips against the solid air.

It is reversal and the backing dark,
The face suspended gazing, recognized,
Lend a sense to spirits which in turn
Dispose the mind to prayer: I press my brow
Against the face in glass which is
Cold as I shall be in death — but moves:
And motion is the ground of hope,
Self the ground of love, and an empty house.

ADAM

Desire stayed with me long after you'd gone.
How long? An hour or two. I went to sleep,
And into sleep it followed me, we followed
Each echoing corridor in search of you.

Desire woke with me and all day it clings
— A shadow cast before which even noon
Does not erase. I pace the long garden
To and fro between box-wood and rose.

I name my little trees, the oak and beech,
The willow, apple, sycamore — all planted close.
I name such blossoms as I know: the lilac,
The honeysuckle with its hint of flesh,

The poppy holding up nine heads, one fractured
Into a flare of red, the others tight still;
Veined irises I name, geum and pansy.
I turn to flowerless plants and name the yew.

Desire has gathered pollen for its use.
Night settles on us in the scented air.
I stand exhausted as after long labour,
Naming each growing thing, not to name you.

ARIEL

If I should touch her, even tenderly,
She would not feel, but if I gave her gifts
These she would accept as from the air
And not suspect me. I would be suspected,
Be seen, and not a temperature she moves through,
Be held, and on her lips
Not ghost of a sound but an articulate word.

CALIBAN

Me she averts her gaze from, me she turns
Into a beast with the pulsing wand of her body.
I bring her acorns and she thanks the trees.
In her I have invested hours of eyes,
Each hour she grows more hard and will be stone.
Then I shall love her in my own time, singing,
She'll not say no, I shall warm her in the sun.

HABIT

Accustomed as I am to ghosts, how could
I recognize, when stretching out my hand,
You were the one that memory could not kill,
Desire would not appal but draw?

Desire, when answered, momentarily alters
To fear, as a match struck in the dark
Animates the shadows we carry
So that they flicker and we shadow them.

Why talk of shadows a body casts?
Think of those that move within, the heart
Throbbing like a bruise and audible
But never to be seen. Imagine it

A Tyrian iris in a wooded place:
Give it a name, but it will not be tended;
It has frail rules of growth, its air, regardless,
A single treasure lost in a starless soil —

Or found. Stretching a hand
Towards the stem of the imagined bloom
I discover a thing tangible,
Clothed in Tyrian fabric, mine in a wooded place.

I had hope of earth, all planted here
With firs and blue pines, evergreens —
Nothing deciduous, no ostentatious flower,
The slow hope with solid trunk and bark.

I had hope of flesh and gave it root.
There is a yield to come. Love needs a home.
If hope finds words, they issue in a prayer.
What answers prayer? What blesses beyond growth?

In the sin that set the firebrand at the gate
I walk out as if naked, calling God.
My forest is now literal, the trees
Rain needles down, but my skin has grown hard.

I lie where I could dream. Today I see
Boughs, and boughs above them, then the sky
Creatured, birds and gnats, a leaping squirrel.
I can no longer read boughs as a map

That guides my wandering upward to a throne.
Having to make and not to find a home,
I am come into man's estate and seek —
Without a child's eye or its appetite

But lumbering, as if ballasted with crime —
God and the garden as incarnate facts —
But facts do not flow to me except this:
I am loved here, when I seek love elsewhere.

1

Whom shall I invite? The centrepiece
Is five red apples on a walnut dish.
The table takes their sheen. Whom
Shall I invite to what the trees provide?

2

Before I choose a guest I go outside.
It is evening almost, almost winter here:
Under the apple tree a pungent mud of fruit,
One bough fractured by the wealth it bears.

3

I have chosen. And will she come?
It is like necromancy to invite
The guest who yesterday, the day before,
Laughing, turned to darkness at my board.

4

Absence I will invite. I will invite
The morning birds, and I will not ask her.
The birds will not come, and she will not come.
The sheen will pass from fruit into the dark.

5

It is too late to eat, too late to ask.
I shall say grace but break no bread.
The lamp will not be lit; I shall sit still
As shadow takes the taste instead.

6

Here is my bed. How the scent of apples clings
To my breathing, and the scent of her.
I am alarmed
How nothing leaves me, though the light is gone.

JACOB

When the meteor was an ignited angel screaming
From the deck of heaven to a darkened trough of flame,
I did believe, my dry lips stuttered, praying
Of love, but the thick tongue was fear; I learned
The ten commandments before my middle name.
One angel burned; another, tumbling, burned.

Red sky... red sky. How well I understood
Sin's gravity, the tug of love between
Light and the dark lapping flames. I was so good,
Good as a saint, truthful, earnest, meek;
God tallied my hairs, he promised food.
They beat me only once or twice a week.

As I grew taller and the stars came near
The heaven I believed in sailed away
For ever, and the angels with it. Meteor
Was only iron, hurled from nowhere to the ground.
The promised food was savourless. I pray,
Lips closing on the silence they have found.

My garden's not much larger than it was
When I was shorter than the dripping jasmine.
My son tries to bottle fireflies, turns his
Clear eyes on earth, on leaves. The heavens fall
About me; but for him, the scent of jasmine,
Jasmine and grace, fireflies, camomile.

OBJECTIONS
for C.H. Sisson

And of that trust you seeded in your garden —
When you walk out one morning on to frost,
Leaves fisted, fruit stony under foot,
Will this differ from the treachery of
The gradual ice that overturned the hewn
Stone of church, the cottages, scattered
Daily from the giant tree of language
All its foliage over an equal lawn?

Eye and heart battened on a mean
Ground which then lost its specific voice.
Every god, the big and small — each local spirit —
Moved off elsewhere, nowhere, night by night.

The way the things that made you let you go
By going off themselves, by simple death —
Is this more unkind than December
Among the twigs and switches of your trees,
Or by the pond where now your fish are stilled
In glass, but at thaw will revolve
And offer eye-white bellies to your eye?

VIGIL
for my son Charles

Sun bleeds through the fleece.
No white or blue in that dawn.
The boy on his rosy sheets
Sleeps and is mine for a time.

In his face I describe
The likenesses in him
To my father and to me
Until we are for a time

Beads on a single thread.
How to give it a name?
The living and the dead —
He wakes for a time

Troubled by my frown:
Sadness or displeasure?
'Those are lines of wonder,'
I want to say, 'for a time.'

Instead I work a smile
Into the glowing room.
He turns his face to the wall
And is erased for a time.

> *My son walked in the green*
> *Light of a million leaves*
> *Until he came to the tree*
> *And hung there for a time.*

My son's chest rises, falls,
He sleeps at the red gates
Of reason, love, and faith
Undreaming, for a time.

RECOVERY
for my daughter Isabel

She's cutting teeth. They come
In a week, a month, the words
Will follow them in her mouth
Until it can make a song.

I think she has returned
From a long stay in the dark
With Dis, and now she cries
For hurt things she saw there.

Feed her the light
Fluids of your blood!
She relearns how to laugh
And memory grows short.

After the teeth, the words,
The song and the stumbling dance,
She will again be a girl
Desired by the dark gods.

This time, may she be strong,
One hand in yours, one in mine,
The serpent under my heel,
The flowers held fast in your palm.

THE HIGH ROOMS
for Claire

Night rain turned the slates to scales, in wind
The roofs became the breathing sides of fish.
Open the freckled window! On the tongue
The drops fell gritty, sour for a time.
But as the air was washed they became sweet.
Your face shone with the white lights from the street.

Tonight's rain is unlike that storm, the place
Has no view but dark hills, viscous sky. Asleep,
Two children; at the skylight our four eyes
Watch not spots of water but a rippling flood
Across the pane, washing a dry reflection.
Watching ourselves, we make the same connection

With that hot evening that the rain turned cool,
The little room behind us, the enormous bed,
Before we were quite comfortable with silence,
Behaving still like strangers strangely lost
In an accidental sacrament, who stare
At one another, at the bolted door.

from
Bedlam & the Oakwood
(1970)

Shallows. Deep, the deep-sea tugging seaweed,
seaweed curling currents on her fingers. How
should I reveal? Between latitude slats the world
looks up, stalks its names and mountains behind bars.

Icebergs, one again last night, burst the diagrammatic
ocean, catch a river mouth and choke the water back on
the blue land: then shifting, melt to green.

This is too cold, too pastel. The world would contour,
my pencil smooths it down. It would make peninsulas
be faces, toes, or fists — some evidence that men
inhabit there. I keep to the rules, manipulating

my latitudes to cut long names, eye-spots of large
cities into halves. The smoke I breathe out circumscribes
my patch of globe, which struggles as I trace.

No men are visible, and what they did
or do is letters only, salted on the land. My smoke
irritates Cuba, Mexico, the Caribbean. My pencil pays
no toll, wanders each road unafraid of bandits, prisoners.

Shutters against Summer,
chairs under sheets, and an all-
yellow garden. I have touched only
the writing desk and stool.
Outside, the gold rose, its teeth
hung on a stem. The sea.

Dim must: gasp
and the bamboo fans
have not air enough
to give you breath. Tonight
stars pump an atmosphere of sea-rose.

Here as blue oysters we characters
are open to an irritant that fails us.
Occasionally we achieve a petulant sublime.

Below, the old sea-keeper
sleeps beside his sea, his hull
carrying coral troves deeper.
As we sat talking
our spirits went to bed.

Voices all night cherish
one another side by side
and never touching. Don't,
for you cannot, follow the spirits
to sleep, or touch them.
Beauty and they are the sea-bed.

Faience is walked colourless
down central corridors, the red and yellow
marrow of the flowers, dull. Through a cloister
and a fountain of raw gold-fish, light passes
in its sharp and silver forms that blind
the things they touch. Even in the long
mummy-room, through a high window,
light, transfixing an old exhibition.

A mother superior in sack-cloth, who appears
to have been corpulent has fallen forwards,
her face rests against the glass.
The body did not suffer until now, prevented
from acacias it admired and would have fed.
Choiring still, dead mouths hang always open
in an O as lips dry back on bone.

This lady of no skin but parchment eyeholes,
and the writing all in age, is called Carmen,
after the convent saint, or Latin song
the birds still make on faded tile.
Now the mouth that Ave'd, like a sucker
holds to the glass,
like the mouth of a fish, for sunlight.

Momentum makes an empress. Work! Forget the heart,
the heart, those palaces and parks of Europe.
'We of the new world build a modern empire. Our formal
gardens undertake the unpatterned shade of big trees,
native flowers beaked and taloned like wild birds.'

Power rose in her, its tulip cupped her heart —
unscrupulous but beautiful; and swans
mated on the lake, thrusting their magnificence
among pleasure boats. What did Cleopatra have
on this? — except a pyramid.

Peace in a barbaric country was not simply come by.
Recurrent measles (the pox, of course) took
imported courtiers, even for a time great
Maximilian. But one accomplishes
moments in the shade like calm.

My devil touches yours here, my hand the stone
you hold over generations. But even now
the devil longs for peace too imperial:
each Indian cowers to uphold it, and you —
invisible ghost rumoured within stone walls.

I missed my train. At least
I didn't miss the journey home,
but waited an hour for the six o'clock.

In that time, I sat conceiving how Ulysses,
missing boats at every port, had ten years
of this. I organized his progress in my eye:

the Troy he left, forever ugly ashes;
breathless women, sorceresses, strewed
his homeward route like petals after wind;

Ithaka so changed, at first a dog alone
recognized him through the smell of oceans,
recalled the tract of time, and died.

Those harbours were not —
he had forgotten — all air and sun,
but stone,

unfriendly ships and storms moored there.
Penelope, at least, perched faithfully like some
grey amorous bird in the famous wedding tree.

When I had seen him through,
for half an hour I prepared a private Odyssey
of my eye. Like the frog,

I thought how blinking I could send
my eye deep, to investigate
my own Mediterranean.

I sing its climb from the hideous
citadel above the nose; its course
through the oesophagus

past the crashing cords that make the voice,
its sojourn with an alveolar Circe
in breezes of the lung, and finally

its shocking Ithaka, it reached
the heart where no one was at home.

from
Desert of the Lions
(1972)

UNDERWATER

Underwater, this is the cathedral
sea. Diving, our bubbles rise
as prayers are said to do, and burst
into our natural atmosphere —
occupying, from this perspective,
the position of a heaven.

The ceiling is silver, and the air
deep green translucency. The worshippers
pray quietly, wave their fins.
You can see the colour of their prayer
deep within their throats: scarlet, some,
and some fine-scaled vermilion; others

pass tight-lipped with moustaches
trailing and long paunches, though
they are almost wafer-thin seen sideways,
or unseen except for whiskers.
Further down, timorous sea-spiders
slam their doors, shy fish disappear

into their tenement of holes, and eels
warn that they have serpent tails.
Deep is wild, with beasts one meets
usually in dreams. Here the giant octopus
drags in its arms. We meet it.
We are hungry in the upper air, and you

have the sea-spear that shoots deep;
you fire accurately, raising a conflagration
of black ink. The animal grabs stone
in slow motion, pulls far under a ledge
and piles the loose rock there as if
to hide might be enough. It holds tight,

builds sanctuary, and I think cries
'sanctuary!' — it dies at your second shot.
We come aboveboard then, with our eight-armed
dinner and no hunger left, pursued by the bland
eyes of fish who couldn't care, by black
water and the death we made there.

He left the room abruptly
dreaming, on a horse.
Still in bed of course
he rode, rode to the sea.

Behind him, his life strung
mile-lengths of wire back
over sand to a shack
where a telephone rang

unanswered. At the sea-side
water made no sound.
Deaf conches strewed the sand.
Seabirds on still air rode

above giant turtles, thick
headed, like fists or a thought.
Silence caught:
the rider could not come back.

His wife murmured in sleep
a dream he did not own.
In its moon-cradle his sin
slept its tiny clenched sleep.

The sea, silent and plain,
lay like a field of weed.
He dismounted and did
what a man will do in pain.

He took off coat and shirt.
He took off skin and bone.
He spread them out on stone:
rose, hyacinth, and heart.

SCORPION
for John Schmidt

Under its stone, it pleats
and unpleats ebony, it digs
a bed which is a body-print
exactly, room for pincer, tail
and sting. If it elbows out, it leaves
cold accurate evidence of its tenancy.

Bedded with it, less precise,
the ambling grubs and slow-worms
eat and burrow deep sometimes
as earthworms, not disturbing that
fast eel of their element — for it
has eyes or nerves that flinch

malignantly at a grain's shift.
I follow you hunting with jar and trowel,
with gloves, this poison tail.
Each time you turn the right stone up —
warm flat stones which roof
an airless square of dark

and hold all night the sun's warmth
for the black king-pin of the poor soil.
The stone raised, the creature poises
tense and cocked. Tail curled, it edges
forward, edges backward — its enemy
so big he is invisible (though a child)

hunched over it, who trembles too
at such a minute potency.
And you flick it with the trowel
into the jar, where it jerks and flings
its fire in all directions at hard
transparency. It asks no mercy.

You bear it to an anthill,
tip it on the dust. Like a cat
it drops right side up, into a tide
of sharp red pincers. It twitches
its tail to a nicety and twice
stings itself — to death. Piece by piece

it is removed underground by the ants —
a sort of burial — perhaps to be
reassembled as a kingly effigy
somewhere deeper than we care to think
bound homeward with our empty jar:
and the field, full of upturned stones.

'INDIAN-PIPES' ARE FLOWERS

at the Desierto de los Leones

In this sort of forest, the bent
pink Indian-pipes all day in drizzle
are puffing mist; and through pines,
as if on damp fire, the monastery smokes,
tall above catacombs, black,
moss-grown, with absent bells.

Monks took the choice spots,
but sent to Spain reports of arid
desert retreats, implying dangerous lions
were about. This desert provided
ample peace to bring off Inquisitions
without prurient eyes. Here, bound,

Indians who could not say the Creed
were brought for instruction, with them
their mild gods of furrow, maize —
exorcised, and only the birds knew.
Indian bones were buried always outside
consecrated ground, not deep.

Those monks learned to construct
a garden where they could relax
after the arduous duties of faith:
zinnia, primula, chrysanthemum and rose
run wild now with a native inspiration,
but then were trellised, chastised into flower.

Within the outlying buildings where we walk
stand posts of body-height,
cut with marks of rope. Minute red poppies
everywhere, recent, like blood-seed,
are spilled, reeking of earth —
the bones of rodents too.

Indians don't come now to pick
mushrooms or sleep in the ghostly lap
of this pine forest — only
vesper swallows home to silence.
Monks preferred the birds to anything.

Spit down this long well-
shaft sounds like a drum-beat,
deep. Water is stone-dark
down there, stone still.
Even the graves we dig don't
go so close to silence.

The Indians nowadays still
put jade pearls in one another's
mouths and leap from high
well-lips like this to reach
'the bone and body of night' —
not here, but north among

the churchless thicket of Kabah.
We salvage their ancestors
by dredging: bone and moss,
beads, clay figurines. Two hands
bound still with threads
of sisal rope we brought up —

took a cast of them before
they dried to dust. I wonder
how they feel, hand in hand,
when water snaps
over their heads and takes
their pearls, lets them

bound together drift to ledges
deeper than our thought,
to lie forever touching, touched
by blind fish and minute fresh
water crab? Bone on bone,
prayed to and envied by the tribe.

We people of the upper air:
our sacrifice of spit is all
the water claims of us. We steal
its pearls and analyse its bones.
It clots our pumps each day
with blue-gilled, eyeless fish.

from
My Brother Gloucester
(1976)

THE JUDAS FISH

I wake to this bewilderment —
my porthole's gone under, the sea flows
too high tonight, and trickles in.
It is not rain, but wind that lifts
and leaves it hovering.

Moments pass without the sky at all.
I share the water-dark that is a sound
intimately chilling, like a voice that whispers
from the world a charm into a dream.
Through the latched porthole

the gentle bleeding from the sea
will be tomorrow a salt web across the floor.
I light my lamp against the starless voice.
It is my face that looks me in the eye.
I cup my hands, look closer

through the face into a shallow pool of light.
A fish might take the porthole for a mild
luminous fish-eye; a night diver
might spot it from a distance as a coin,
antique, the frail imperial face

on alloyed gold, wide-eyed,
not negotiable, gazing
into the marches around empire
where froth is the untouchable barbarian.
Looking out, indeed, there is not much to see,

no diver, no near fish, nothing
to crave possession over,
though there is a strange
possessiveness in water, as in sunlight,
determining the shadows. Water casts up

shadows of a curious kind, swirling
three inches from the eyes — an impulse
to undo the latch for once, gingerly
to invite oblivion in,
let the driving current touch and have its way.

Yet it is a driven current at the pane
that has claimed as many histories as time
and planted them in beds of sand and coral,
in thicket weeds, in feeding of its fish;
its fluid memory retains suspended

elements of mountains, ships and mariners
unredeemable as salt within the blood,
but present: the dead are tasted
like rich sediment, flooding
the secret latitudes.

Subsiding with the wind the water goes,
my porthole fills with constellations
that never touched a life,
and they are welcome, identifiable —
although before they came back I believe

a fish pulsed into view in the dwindling water
with thirty silver scales upon its side
and a Judas eye trained on me, focusing.
I slipped the latch then.
It was starlight that came in.

The cone-snail shrinks from us.
Its mouth is sealed.
Nothing will tempt it out again
but washing in the sea. It is cast up.
We gather it with shells and take it home.

Of all that we collected it is this
we look at first. It's edged with tiny stings.
We set it on the floor
and bring the reading glass to make it large.
It leaks a yellow liquid like a wound.

In the lip there is a rim of glyphs.
They are crimson on pearl white, each
distinctly written, like a text we magnify.
These tendril lines are veins
that bear poison to the stings.

If we knew how to read
we could not deny a language here.
The fluent tracery is more
than a snail articulating vanity:
it is a charm to keep its body whole.

An eyeless thing
fingering with blunt horns
the walls it grew, gradually
sketched these images,
translating them by instinct into shell;

it was a jelly substance working sand,
fitting itself to sand and sand to it,
observing the reciprocal slow laws
to make its long vault issue from the heart
up to the lips and there describe these symbols.

We cannot pry open the fixed mouth.
Does the writing continue in the throat,
through the length of the deep whorl, until
at the core the riddle is resolved?
We tap it. It fractures like egg-shell.

In the innermost recess the snail has shrivelled
hard as a pea. We are deceived:
the vaults are white throughout,
and what there was to say was clearly
written on the lips and spoken there.

WORDS
after Hofmannsthal

Child, your eyes will darken soon with wonder —
and darken ignorantly till they're blind.
We will pass by you as we were passed by.

The fruit is bitter. It will sweeten in the dark
and drop into your hands with broken wings.
Cherish it a day. But it will die.

The wind comes down to you from history.
It chilled us too. The phrases it repeats
are stale with pleasure, stale with punishment.

The paths lead from the garden to the world,
to places where light burns among the trees
that raise their wings but cannot hope to fly.

Who cast the root of everything so deep
that nothing flies away that we can name?
Why can we laugh and in a moment cry

and give a name to laughter and to tears?
What is the illness that our eyes grow dark?
— We are men because we are alone:

we touch and speak, but silence follows words
the way a shadow does, the hand draws back.
The curtain blows and there is no one there.

What removed you to this solitude,
into this common light, this common twilight?
It is that word, twilight, that called you down —

a word the wind has handed on to us
undeciphered, and it might be love —
rich with a honey pressed from hollow combs.

It is as though the whole town is on ice.
Skaters with a speed of birds
greet each other on reflected cloud
mid-stream, up-stream, past the crippled boats.
There is a horse and sledge.
A bonfire burns its censer shape into the cold.
Someone sells grilled fish

again today, for it's been weeks
the river froze, and a man dared
walk out on the water.
No one has looked back since:
ice-fishermen with saw and string,
the schools of children, the slower
shopkeepers like large sedate fish.

The habitual town has ceased. It's chosen
another better world, a world of days
prayed for, persistent beyond hope,
a flowering of impossibilities.
Buildings line the shore
derelict like plundered sea-chests
and the pirate is the ice.

I tie on my skates and find the air
moves me like a feather from the shore.
I leave town for the frozen falls.
I fly up-stream like a salmon, light
with spawn. I come home
and pass by for the sea, and turn again.
Sun sparks my blades, I send up

grit of ice like quick flame.
I burn my hours religiously,
my ceremony to the ice and air.
But today the air is warmer, our days
are numbered. The falls are dripping
and the sea barks and barks
into the brittle river mouth. It is like

sailing at the end of a brief world, beyond
responsibility, and time is purposeless,
pure of daily history and bread.
To put on wings is an authentic dream, and yet
up on shore the dirtied nest of facts
is patient in the sun, tall and lowering
above the vistas of the heart,

and even now beneath the ice
the other world continues
undisturbed, the weeds are spun by currents,
the pearls increase to buy our future eyes;
the small fish feed, are fed on, the great
round-eyed flounder old as water
subsist on certainties among stilled keels
and out to sea, by rough boulders and the light,
the wrecked laden hulls, the mariners . . .

If the inhabitants of that world look up
they perceive hairline cracks
fissuring the ice
and our veined shadows pass
against the light like baits
they will not take, but wait —
cold acolytes, whose business is
each candle and the dark.

THE FOOL

I warn you, said the Fool,
I have a job to do. I do it well.
I am the lowest rung on the man ladder;
my place, unchallenged, is not inconvenient

for I look up and undersee your polished boots
holed through utterly beneath, your hosiery
tattered at the knee, and you in silks outside
below are bare as apricots, as radishes.

Your bodies' downward scent is unperfumed.
I smell your misdemeanours and your motives.
— Yet every heart beats only from my heart
if it beats truly, though no voice speaks

my language. None speaks truly.
In my rhetoric I am in the earth the undertaker,
the first worm who bears the licensed key
and unlocks every body: mine

is the first taste, my certificate
implies a corpse impure enough to plunder.
I am the deepest, oldest, thinnest fish
upon the seabed in the rocks and sand:

I see the world entire in glancing up,
I intercept and touch the whale's long sound,
the prim sea-horse I watch grow old and faithless,
the sallow bladder-fish inflate and fawn

on sleek sea-kale trees that stand up like kings.
And yet I have no name but my two eyes,
my speech that none replies to,
a venerable, antique uniform.

I have — I'm had on sufferance.
I am afraid of dark as much as you.
I pull my cap across my eyes and sleep.
I dream of an ignorant and sunny kingdom

trivial, passionate, where all have hearts
within undisfigured bodies that are breathing
like men and women coming out of marble
into an actual day, as fish move out from weeds

blinking at the galleons that sink
and break before them on the seabed, spilling
treasure meaningless and brilliant, habitable;
and the drowned mariners more slowly drifting
touch down as gently dead as leaves.

THE ENGLISH LESSON
after Pasternak

When it was Desdemona's turn to sing
and only minutes of her life remained,
she did not mourn her star, that she had loved:
she sang about a tree, a willow tree.

When it was Desdemona's time to sing,
her voice grew deeper, darker as she sang;
the darkest, coldest demon kept for her
a weeping song of streams through rough beds flowing.

And when it was Ophelia's turn to sing
and only minutes of her life remained,
she was dry as light, as a twig of hay:
wind blew her from the loft into the storm.

And when it was Ophelia's time to sing,
her dreams were waning, all but the dream of death.
Bitter and tired — what tokens sank with her?
In her hair wild celandine, and willows in her arms.

Then letting fall the rags of human passion,
heart-first they plunged into the flowing dark,
fracturing their bodies like white tinder,
silencing their unbroken selves with stars.

THE SLEIGH
after a theme of Turgenev

The colours have gone out.
It is like death — blind white
and the sun is white: we speed
the way we always wished —
a sleigh, the harness bells — across the snow.

It's not what we expected.
Afraid on the ice road
we ring to the empty farms
that we've come their way but not to stop.
Who set the burning pennies on our eyes?

Think — if the runners struck a rut
and hurled us into temporary graves
face-down like heretics; or if the jingling
ceased and we flew silently
on into the open throat of night.

Speed and the snow
blend field and hedge and landmark
in one whiteness like a future.
Perhaps the thaw will turn it up like new —
and yet we cannot see that far today.

Under the arcane dunes
suppose the past is unreclaimable
too truly for March sun and its tired miracle.
What if a half-hearted wish for warmth
is all we bring ourselves, and bring no love

hot to melt the things it cannot love?
What if we trust all changes to the snow?
I think the snow will see us off:
we're going to die
whirling, two flakes

of headlong colour
over the unmarked brink.
In a flash of white, as though we are to hang,
we shall relive our separate short lives.
— We have not touched or taken

the feather weight of pain.
If it was war, then we were traitors there.
If it was famine, we ate on and on; and now
we're turned to cowards in a day we owned,
returned as serfs to fields we ruled as czars,

we plough the snow where once
we led the hunt through hedge and stream-bed
up to the lodge and there were ladies there.
It is neglect and snow leave open graves
we ride from to worry at a world

we partly chose, and where
forgetfulness makes easy graves we go
across a brilliance like purity
to no known place.
The driver turns and points but we are blind.

I dread a destination and the thaw
that will set us down and leave us to ourselves
as we are now. We are
the dying penitent who feels too late
the cold breath of the beggar on his hand.

I wish I could look on
rather than be here a piece of blindness.
I would not call
to those who go together
and seem upon the snow as cold as snow,

but from a distant cottage I would watch
a tiny horse advance
with a faint pulse of bells
drawing its burden, as a spider draws a fly
across its web of light into the dark.

for N.E. Gorbanevskaya,
detained in prison mental hospital

Her heart peers out
between her breathing shoulder-blades:
curious, fist-sized.

It gazes down the spine
as down a highway. From its high vantage
it observes unbroken snow,

the broken slumber, broken snow.
Under glacial contours of the skin
the lakes persist, dilate; the rivers

irrigate so deep cartographers ignore them.
Aya, Raya, her Estonian names
conjure their villages,

the farmers who received her
in their houses and their language:
how they are squinting,

blinded by their fields of snow,
how the one road leads
one way and loses them.

There, at the highway's end,
Tartu, a pole of exile.
Here, between the shoulders,

the other pole of exile is the heart —
renewing the old journeys
with each syllable of pulse —

until it flickers like a candle, votive,
ignited to the guardian of exiles,
shadowed out by the twin blades of bone.

She wakes to the ward smell
and sound of other dreaming,
in a frayed prison smock, in the early light;

to her face reflected from the dusty pane:
a face of Russia with no caption, with no
black border, no number and no name.

It was the fruit I wanted, not the nest.
The nest was hanging like the richest fruit
against the sun. I took the nest

and with it came the heart, and in my hand
the kingdom and the queen, frail surfaces,
rested for a moment. Then the drones

awoke and did their painful business.
I let the city drop upon the stones.
It split to its deep palaces and combs.

It bled the insect gold,
the pupa queens like tiny eyes
wriggled from their sockets, and somewhere

the monarch cowered in a veil of wings
in passages through which at evening
the labourers had homed,

burdened with silence and the garden scents.
The secret heart was broken suddenly.
I, to whom the knowledge had been given,

who was not after knowledge but a fruit,
remember how a knot of pains
swelled my hand to a round nest;

blood throbbed in the hurt veins
as if an unseen swarm mined there.
The nest oozed bitter honey.

I swaddled my fat hand in cotton.
After a week pain gave it back to me
scarred and weakened like a shrivelled skin.

A second fruit is growing on the tree.
Identical — the droning in the leaves.
It ripens. I have another hand.

THE SHELLS
a guided tour in the Andes

These shells are from no familiar sea —
they litter furrows in the mountain fields.
Ploughing turns them over year to year.
They come back more predictably than maize:

almost ordinary, like a worker's bruised nails,
but inside luminous in certain lights
as mother pearl. They are stone now. The plough
can chip them but they are the years':

they do not break outright.
When these mountains were lifted from the sea
they carried the live cities of the sea —
the scallop beds, the clams in families

fisted on to marl, and sand a pure
salt white. The water rilled away; the salts
have worked their passage back to water.
The shells stayed until they are these stones

among farmers who have never seen the sea
or tasted fish, who plough with wood
and weed by hand and touch them as elaborate
queer flints or coloured stones.

This is what time does when history
leaves it to itself — retrieves organic
monuments for a longer eternity than ours —
these mute informers that are twice over

stone: of memory and stone. We might
stop here a day and gather them
as Darwin did in sacks, to ship home
for minute interrogation. We might spend

an hour with the Indian farmers
to whom we are enigmas, rich and pale,
and tell them how the fine-lipped shells,
the delicate bright eyes of soil are not

real stone, how these coarse fields
plunder a dead sea city that —
if they knew its language —
could rob them of their given catechism.

Better leave them be, each to his field,
ploughing securely towards their seventh day.
We have our own sufficient luggage
of broken promises and curios for home.

The bus is waiting and our tribe is tired.
We'll keep a secret they could not believe
and let the shells be turned and turned for seasons
as the unspent coins of passage out of faith.

We can't sleep tonight. The ice has formed —
from thin skin at evening
to deep stone. With midnight
the boat's aground in it.
Planks shriek against the hardening.

Below deck a film of frost pales everything.
Our breath makes beads of ice. We pace
between the hatch and bunks.
The world would end by ice
tonight, for sure, if we lay down.

Come outside: the wind has sculpted
sails to marble drapery;
on the line our laundry freezes to
a rigor mortis of our bodies' clothes.
Night will hardly darken all this glass —

the stars are treble on its rippled plane.
Birds stiffen on the surface,
bellies up, like fish.
We started from a tropic on whose shore
the lizards' tongues were flames of malachite

in leaves that trailed on to the tide,
and crimson fish were couriers there
to caverns where eels uncoiled their sting.
Night plankton burned our wake —
for years we have been heading north.

When lips are tucked away for good
and rigid as ice-starched shirt and trousers
we pass the climax of our slow miasma,
and the river hardens in the arteries
till the heart with the hull surrenders

to stillness and is broken like a stone,
when our histories are minuted, adjourned,
our faces upturned to a Sabbath star,
this will be the scene if we can see,
the fish arrested with the drifting tyres,

the dry snow driven into dunes of ash.
It was not like this in the other place —
there all was fire and water,
nothing stilled the waves
that might be furious though they never died

to the intolerable vacancy
we pace to keep the blood awake. Come down.
We'll light the burner, thaw our fingers out.
We are the ashes that will cover us,
our inch of life, our mile, our field of breathing.

from
A Change of Affairs
(1978)

A DREAM
        for C.H. Sisson

I had a dream on good authority
That fastened on me like a stitch in skin:
Construct a boat, God said, *along these lines*
And spread the plan out on his cloudy knee.

So many cubits wide, and here the masts,
And make the hull as large as a hotel.
The animals, of course. Reptiles? and bugs?
Each animal, and two of those in love.

There will be forty nights without a star
And forty days go by without a sun
And when the clouds break there will be nowhere
Till oceans find another hemisphere.

That dream is some time past. The fields are full
Of grain, the mating creatures now give birth.
I come home evenings a puzzled man,
Hearing the infants cry, touching the solid earth.

I tell the dream and reason thus with Shem:
'Dear boy,' I say, 'if we construct this thing
The flood may come and we will be the cause.
God does not act until his will is done.'

'The earth will all be ours, though,' says Shem:
'Imagine, all the ground from here to night,
And God will fix his eye on us alone
And make our offspring rich, our furrows full.'

Japheth is lazy. When I worry him
He says, 'Let's have it built, then we can sleep
For forty days under the care of God
And settle later in a quiet grove.'

Ham is a craftsman, handy with a saw.
I hardly told the dream when he began
Pricing old planks and readying his tools.
He worries me, his eye on destiny.

Shem tallies, Japheth dreams, and Ham prepares.
Our neighbours have heard nothing though the wave
Hangs over them and I could make it break.
I don't believe the dream was meant for me.

THE BROTHER

Why is his sacrifice
More suitable than mine?
I give the grain I've sown
And he, sheep from his flock.
Mine is a laboured gift,
His a giving back.

It is not what I give —
Rather, my shape you despise.
You light his flame to see
A body nicely formed
For sitting on a hill
Above a bleating flock
And playing on a reed
A parody of praise.

You make my flame slow
And smokier than light.
My arms and legs are scarred
From moving in sharp grass.
I am no idol for
The god who made the snake
Or the abhorrent tree.
My praise is in the field
Enacting punishment.

If beauty's not my tithe,
But only what I do,
If what I am attracts
No more than a slow flame,
I know what I can kill
To draw your eye to me.

It's Absalom who mouths the famous prayer —
'David, David, father, O my father' —
Meanwhile his father king is treading air,
A fist of twigs has clutched him by the hair;
He walks and walks, the tree won't let him down —
It holds the head although it lost the crown.
The air is cooler when the sun has spilled
Its cordial red along the sterile hills,
Imbibed the sweat of battle by degrees,
Leaving the salt, the man, the faithful tree.
The son is victor and his golden hair
Lights like a torch the court's grey atmosphere
And for an evening, mourning victory,
Keeps to the forms of grief with a dry eye.
Perhaps I, David, who once bore the head
Of brute Goliath that my stone struck dead,
And freed my people to their wilderness
And made my body their intelligence —
Beautiful, articulate and just — am now
Only a weariness. I see him grow
Into the shadow that time shed from me
As though it suited him; and from this tree
I worship him as my loves worshipped me;
Desire's old logic in a head that's grey,
Gnarled fingers, and the once eloquent heart
Give way like stone the sharp frost cleaves apart
And leaves. I take my human medicine
And do not curse him, my usurping son,
But close my eyes to hold him in my head —
Here in this tree, his lover, hanging dead.

It is a winter sky.
I take a fist of stars —
A hundred if you please —
And seed dark vacancies.

They choose a hundred lands
To throb above.
Each land is cold and yet
Not closed to miracles.

A hundred miracles
Would strain credulity:
If man can love no more
Than once in a blue moon

A God loves his bad world
One time in history
At most, and pours his blood.
He'll come next time as fire.

But in a hundred lands
The shepherds leave their flocks
To seek a manger child
Following my stars.

And in a hundred Easts
The wise men pack their bags
And leave their palaces
And people to the snow.

Each manger's visited.
There's one beneath each star.
There is only one child,
One miracle. One star

Tells the truth and stays.
The others draw their line
And fall into the sea
With their false promises.

The sheep have strayed meanwhile.
The people die of cold.
The shepherds will not stop
Their scrabbling in the straw.

The wise men have not homed.
They wait upon the child
Although he died and rose
Too long ago for love
Except by miracle.

I was simply asleep.
There was a sound in my ear —
A form moved in my tent,
A hammer and a spike.
The spike pricked my brow
And then the hammer fell.

I feel the years. Impaled,
I lie within my tent.
My army dies, the flies
Have come and gone away.

I know who she was.
She may return. I lie still
And do not speak or cry.
I let her do her will.
My name is Sisera.
I will not say her name:
She may still be alive.

Now I have seen the man
   The Manichee I was
Withdraws to the phantom cross
   And hangs in darkness there.

Some part of me is damned
   For ever. Let it go.
The fire will deal with it
   As quickly as a leaf.

I spare that little ash
   And turn to the real flesh.
A man with angel's eyes
   Stands by me with the nails.

He whispers that the beams
   With bark as thick as skin
Will hold my body firm
   As they have held before

Even a man like him
   Who looked with angel's eyes.
I take from his broken hand
   The spikes of paradise.

Until I built the wall they did not find me.
Sweet anarchy! attending quietly
To wild birds or picking the blackberry.

Trespassers did not know they erred and came
In and away, leaving the land the same.
The hunter went to richer ground for game.

Tending, profitless, my property
Which no map mentioned, where no metal lay
In veins beneath the surface of hard clay

And bristle grass, I watched my livestock — scores
Of lizards, armadillos, and the birds —
Free citizens. I had concealed no snares.

Mere ground. Mere nothing harvested or sown.
But how the shadows made the rough design
Live as a landscape for the man alone!

So I grew proud. That's why I built the wall
Of stone and mortar, and I drove a nail
Into a stake and hung a sign to tell

The wanderer *Private Land*, with guarantees
Of instant death for *anyone who tries*
To enter here: leave hope. Vain promises!

Who would I kill or could I kill?
Before I turned a servant of the will
To mark my ground, indeed, who would I hurt or kill?

Now peering from the rim of my high wall
I see the plain outside abruptly shrill
With enemies I do not know. They call

Who's in there, what do you mean, and why?
I hold my peace, but they've discovered me
Because I drew a line, a *Here am I.*

They rob my peace, they take away my sleep.
Their voices drizzle all the night. I step
Along the wall as round a castle keep

Till in the daylight there they stand again,
Drawn up from their shadows till at noon
Ghost warriors hover by the place I own.

As ribs around a heart, the gentle wall
Tucks in the land, or as a crisp snail shell
Cups its soft cause. Yet yearlong vigil

Sours memory of the lovely ground,
Rivets to masonry the heart and hand:
I tend a straitened altitude of stone.

I am like the worm.
Cut in two, I'd thrive.
Within the metaphor
I greet myself, I take
My right hand in my right
And looking eye to eye
I'm satisfied. I need
A knife to make it true,
A simple slice, and clean;
Another lover too.

The worm resembles me.
The rough dark hardens it.
Within the metaphor
It only knows it is
And not which way it goes
To what, from what, how far.
I want a blade to fall
Between me so I move
Forward fore and aft
And double the odds for love.

The worm and I emerge
Into the rainy light.
We wander on the lawn
And lose our entrances.
I kneel on a flagstone
And press it with my thumb.
It twists into a ring
And writhes away again.
Here resemblance ends
Like casual marriages.

You came at evening,
A tardy labourer,
And joined the courtyard full
Of those I'd called between
The hours of six and six.
You had not touched
The vines or turned the soil,
But at the table where
I paid the equal wage
To those whose skin was burned
By a whole day of sun
And those who came at five,
Whose brows were dry of sweat,
You claimed your salary.

And what is due to you —
To those white hands, that face?
What to that bright dress,
The body with its sweet
Scent among reeking flesh?
I make you stand aside
And when the men are gone
I give you what remains:
The trellises and vines,
The hoes and rakes, the keys.
Next day I come at dawn
To work in the hot sun.

'I MAKE NO SECRET OF IT . . .'

I make no secret of it:
Your fish came to my bait
And kissed the hook before I'd fairly cast.
I gave up fishing, but I cannot walk
By water without all those tiny o's
Pocking the surface, like the pores in skin.

WAKING AND SLEEPING

1
I forget which of these plants I planted.
The wind brought some, a few were in the soil.
Better to dig them up and start again
And know the garden when it comes to flower.

But the seeds — I cannot trust or credit
The words on the bright paper pod.
Inside is a sound like sand — dry, credible.
Better a barren patch than unknown harvest.

A barren patch, burnt off, kept dry as cinders,
Protected against rain and from the dew.
Yet it, like any acre, a night neglected,
And there are toadstools the air has made,

Exotic lungs — a nap will foster them.
Even a desert is not sterile soil.
I will give up the plot, give over
The flower, seed, the lungs, the watching over.

2

Being free I am compelled one way:
Down hill, my will exhausted. I decline
Like water around stones into the sea.
But at the shore I pause in time, I turn
And climb the hill again, compelled one way.

Better than up and down, to be a slave
And take direction from a cunning goad,
Or be a puppet that accepts the strings
And always moves secure in law or pain.
Being free, I would elect that course.

But being free denies me that request
And will not let itself exceed its word.
I have no rule but lawlessness, no heart
Except the motor of my pulse; in sleep
My eyes come loose and roll about my skull
Like pearls. I am the doll of anarchy.

PIANO

You can make music come from those cold keys.
Alone and grandly I adjust the stool,
Flap up my shirt tail, take your seat, arrange
Feet on the pedals, poise my hands, then pause.
Around me evening holds its breath.

Accustomed as I am to hear you play,
I hear you with my hands above the keys
And can imagine that I sit apart
Patient, watching your shoulders move
Into the music as a dancer sways,

Your intimacy with a sheet of notes
I can't approach, your feet that press
Gently the brass pedals so they take
A chord as far as you would have it go
Or clear the air of music instantly.

There, your sleeves turned up
To the elbow, and your forearms pale
Above the ivory and the shadow keys
On evenings like this . . . the ghost of you
Compels me to keep silence in your place.

HERE AND THERE

There, you are climbing to the Aber Falls.
Here, at my table, I think of you:
The mist around you and your body's pulse
Makes its own intimate atmosphere
From which you gaze out loving that landscape —
You pass the wild horses and the marsh trees.
Here, beside myself, I follow you.

Last year we went that path in rain and found
The falls come out of cloud, not off a cliff:
A torrent poured by the invisible. We took
Shoes and socks off, waded to the pool.
Slipping, letting go, who cares: in deep
Up to the waist, with the fish, we moved
Under the fall's full weight.
The water struck us like an avalanche.

The weather never cleared. It won't today.
There, now, you may have reached the upper pool.
You may be taking off your shoes and socks.
Here, I flex my toes inside my shoes.
Shall I go take a bath? I ask you:
How to wash this image out, erase
Trees, the hand in hand, the shaft of water,
Its force that knocked me dumb into your arms?

THE HONEYSUCKLE

Your honeysuckle, since you've been away
Breathes heavily. Your room is full of scent.
I look into the dusk. Your labour's there,
The tending that gradually seduced
Soil and stem to render up a pattern.
Your work becomes like theirs, as they reduce
Their straggling to ordered scent and hue,
Hospitable to birds. Your only care
Is measuring of growth, decay; and time
Is seasons of the bud, the withering,
Unabstract, with unspoken promises.

Unbroken, too. Each year the place prepares,
Punished and loved — two passions of one heart —
To give what profit a beloved can give.
You choose that time of year to go,
Leaving to me the climax. I'm not in love
With greenery, but you — and left with what you made
Of a small garden and a broken tree
I fumble with your chores, meek but unbeguiled.

Evening takes off the brilliance by degrees
Until the poppy is a ghost, the rose
A bruise among its foliage; then dark
Fills in the scented trough between the hedges,
Extinguishes the tree, absolves the eye from all
Reality. I lie in your dark room
Intent to think of nothing, sleep.
Only, the honeysuckle comes,
An air that you prepared, to fill your place.